This book belongs to:

..................................................................................

# AUTUMN
## PUBLISHING

Published in 2025
First published in the UK by Autumn Publishing
An imprint of Igloo Books Ltd
Cottage Farm, NN6 0BJ, UK
Owned by Bonnier Books
Sveavägen 56, Stockholm, Sweden
www.autumnpublishing.co.uk

Copyright © 2020 Autumn Publishing

All rights reserved. No part of this publication may be
reproduced or transmitted in any form or by any means,
electronic, or mechanical, including photocopying, recording,
or by any information storage and retrieval system,
without permission in writing from the publisher.

0925 007
4 6 8 10 9 7 5
ISBN 978-1-80368-482-6

With special thanks to consultant Philippa Wilson
Illustrated by Diane Le Feyer

Designed by Justine Ablett
Edited by Stephanie Moss

Printed and manufactured in the EU

# Old Testament

The Creation Story..................................6

Noah's Ark...........................................30

The Tower of Babel..............................54

Abraham and Sarah.............................56

Jacob and Esau....................................58

Joseph and His Coat of Many Colours...62

Moses..................................................86

Moses and the Israelites.....................90

The Israelites Conquer Jericho.........94

The First King of Israel......................96

David and Goliath.............................100

King Solomon...................................104

Daniel and the Lions.........................106

Jonah and the Whale........................110

# New Testament

| | |
|---|---|
| The Christmas Story……………134 | The Hole in the Roof……………184 |
| Jesus Visits the Temple……………158 | The Lost Sheep……………192 |
| Jesus is Baptised……………160 | Zacchaeus……………200 |
| Jesus and His Disciples……………162 | The Prodigal Son……………208 |
| Jesus Feeds 5,000 People……………164 | Jairus's Daughter……………216 |
| Jesus Walks on Water……………166 | Raising Lazarus……………224 |
| The Woman at the Well……………168 | The Easter Story……………232 |
| The Good Samaritan……………176 | |

# The Creation Story

In the beginning, before time began, there was nothing. Nothing to see and nothing to hear. Nothing to touch or smell. There was only silence. God moved alone through the inky darkness.

Then, on the first day, God created the heavens and the Earth, and the Earth was covered by water. "Let there be light," said God. At first, the light was faint. It was a flicker in the darkness that grew brighter and stronger. Then it became a glowing ball that pushed the gloom aside. It was soft and yellow, then red, pink and dazzling gold. God delighted in its loveliness. The changing light seemed to have a life of its own, and God called it 'day'. When the light faded into darkness, He named it 'night'. It was the very first day of the world.

On the second day, when the light came back, God made the sky. It was a soft, bright blue, and it hung over the Earth like a canopy.

On the third day of the world, God pulled back the choppy waters so that the solid ground underneath appeared. He named the great pools of water, which were blue like the sky and shimmering in the light, the 'seas'. He called the big muddy areas of ground 'land'. The land was flat and bare, so God shaped it into mountains, plains and deep valleys. Soon, under His guiding hand, greenery covered the Earth.

## The Creation Story

Grasses and plants of every size, shape and colour began to grow and sweet-smelling flowers blossomed. The sticky buds opened and vines wound into the air. Trees sprang from the ground, their branches reaching for the sky, growing tall and heavy with fruit. The Earth had become lush and green, overflowing with plant life.

On the fourth day, God said, "Let there be signs to mark the day and night." He made the fiery Sun to show the day and the gentle Moon to shine at night. During the day, the Moon hid in the shadows. At night, the Sun turned its golden face away, while the Moon cast its silvery beams over the land.

God also brightened the night sky with millions upon millions of tiny glittering stars. He felt pleased with the beautiful world He had created.

God's new world was a peaceful land filled with flowers, trees and rushing rivers, but there were no birds to perch in the trees. There were no bees to buzz from flower to flower, and no fish to leap through the waves. The only sounds were the whisper of the wind among the leaves and the waves lapping the shores.

## The Creation Story

So, on the fifth day, God filled the sea with living creatures. Suddenly, it was swimming with fish that moved as one. He made whales that sprayed water high up into the sky, and dolphins that leaped playfully in and out of the waves. He made jellyfish that shimmered like moonlight, shellfish that sparkled like precious stones and tiny crabs that waved their claws on the golden sands.

Then God said, "Let there be creatures of the air that will fill the sky with life." Suddenly, there was a great fluttering of feathers and flapping of wings, as birds and insects of all shapes and sizes rose into the sky. Tiny hummingbirds mingled with colourful parakeets and silent, gliding hawks. The sky was alive with colour and sound as the twittering birds found shelter among the trees and bushes. They busied themselves with discovering sweet fruit and washing their feathers in the cool streams. Their happy songs filled God's ears, and He blessed them.

# The Creation Story

On the sixth day of the world, God said, "Now, let there be creatures on the land!" and the Earth began to shake with the thunder of a thousand feet. The world hummed with voices large and small, all trying to be heard. Regal lions prowled beside mighty elephants and rhinos. Monkeys swung through the trees, cackling to each other, and snakes rustled through the undergrowth.

Fierce animals paced side by side with the gentlest of God's creatures. Everyone, from the tiny shrews to the tall giraffes, was looking for a new home. Some liked the cool of the snowy mountains, and some preferred the heat of the rainforests. Cheetahs raced into the jungle, crocodiles hid in rivers, while squirrels climbed tall trees. The world pulsed with life. God looked around and was happy with what He saw. But something was missing.

# Children's Bible Stories

# The Creation Story

"Who will care for all the animals?" God asked Himself. So, He took handfuls of earth and shaped two creatures who looked like Him. He called them 'man' and 'woman'. As God poured His breath into them, the man and woman began to move. They opened their eyes and stared around in wonder. They slowly stretched their arms and legs, and rose to their feet. They stood in front of God, holding hands, as beautiful and innocent as the new world. God blessed them, and named the man Adam and the woman Eve.

"Your job is to look after the wonders I have created," He said. "You will rule over the fish in the sea, the birds in the sky and every creature on the Earth. You will have fruit to eat and water to drink. I want you to enjoy your life here."

# Children's Bible Stories

# The Creation Story

God's work was done. The world was every bit as beautiful as He had imagined. It was the seventh day, and God rested.

CHILDREN'S BIBLE STORIES

# The Creation Story

Next, God made a beautiful garden for Adam and Eve, and named it Eden. There were flowers, trees full of delicious fruit to eat and velvet-soft grass to lie on. A sparkling stream gave Adam and Eve clean water to drink.

There was a huge tree in the middle of the garden. Its branches reached into the sky like upstretched arms, and God named it the Tree of Knowledge. "You can pick fruit from any tree in the garden, except the Tree of Knowledge," He told Adam and Eve. "If you eat from that tree, you will die." Adam and Eve listened to everything God said. They had all that they needed and they were happy. They cared for the animals and the garden, just as God had told them.

# Children's Bible Stories

One day, Eve was picking berries near the Tree of Knowledge when she heard rustling in the leaves of the tree. A snake was watching her, its tongue flicking in and out. "Smell the sweet fruit," the snake hissed. "Try it. *Tassste* it!"

"No," Eve replied. "God has told us we must not eat the fruit from the Tree of Knowledge or we will die."

The snake shook its head. "It would make you as wise as God," it said. "*Jussst* one bite would make you a goddess." The snake's words made Eve long to try it. Slowly, she picked a rosy apple and drew it towards her. It smelled so sweet and delicious. Her heart thumped with fear and excitement. Eve could not resist. She took a tiny bite of the apple.

The Creation Story

Adam saw her and, although he knew that it was wrong, he burned with curiosity. So, Eve handed him the apple and he tried it. Smiling, the snake slithered away. God knew at once what Adam and Eve had done. He was upset and angry. "You must leave Eden," He told them. "From now on, the lives of humankind will be full of trouble and worry. Now that you have eaten from the Tree of Knowledge, your bodies will eventually die. But I will find a way to save you."

Adam and Eve shivered as the gates of Eden clanged shut behind them. Greed had taken them from a place of gentle breezes to a cruel world where the wind blew and the rain soaked their bodies. But God, who loves His people, gave Adam and Eve something very special. He gave them hope. Perhaps one day, He told them, humankind might yet return to the beautiful garden of Eden and to the love of God.

# Noah's Ark

Long ago, when the world was still new, God saw that all was not well. Golden sun still warmed the Earth, silver moonlight lit the nights, and the hills, valleys, rivers and seas were as beautiful as on the day God made them. But the world had changed. The people had become wicked. They hurt one another and caused trouble. They had forgotten that God wanted them to be good. In fact, they had forgotten Him completely. Seeing this made God so unhappy that He wished He'd never made people. He decided that something must be done.

As God looked down on the world, His eyes fell upon one man called Noah. He was the only man on Earth who remembered God. He worked hard every day, although he was an old man. Noah's wife, three sons and his son's wives all worked hard, too. They were happy, kind to each other and good to their neighbours, even though they received no kindness in return. They lived a good life, and it was the sort of life God had hoped all people would live when He created them.

# Children's Bible Stories

# Noah's Ark

God was pleased with Noah and his family. He decided that they deserved to live on Earth and He would protect them. But everyone else had been wicked, and they could not be saved. God told Noah about His plan to change the world. "The world is full of evil," God said, "so I am going to send a great flood to wash it clean. Nearly everyone and everything will be wiped away, apart from you and your family, Noah. The world will begin again, as fresh and good as when it was first created, and you and your family will live there."

Noah was very frightened. "What must I do?" he asked, trembling. "You should build an ark," said God. "It must be big enough to hold two of every animal in the world, one male and one female, and food for all of them. It must be strong, because it will be battered by the floodwaters for many days."
"I will do exactly as You say," said Noah. He was glad that he and his family would be saved from the flood, but he was sad about what would happen to the world and all the other people, and worried about what God had told him to do.

"How can I build such an ark? I'm not a shipbuilder," thought Noah. "And how can I collect so many animals? God expects so much of me and I'm afraid I will fail." But God wouldn't let Noah fail. He was there beside Noah every step of the way, helping him and telling him what to do. Noah and his sons worked hard, chopping, sawing, sanding and hammering until gradually, the ark took shape.

# Noah's Ark

While Noah worked, God spoke to him. "It will rain for 40 days and 40 nights, and the land will be covered with water. But you, Noah, will be safe in the ark."

As Noah and his sons worked, their neighbours watched from a distance. "What are you doing, Noah?" they asked, laughing at him. "Why do you need a boat when the sea is miles away?" Noah heard them laughing, but he didn't listen.

After many weeks, the ark was finished. It was taller, longer and stronger than any boat there had ever been. It was smooth and shiny on the outside, with strong shutters at the windows and heavy locks on the door. It was the perfect boat for stormy weather. There were lots of rooms inside, some wide enough for the largest pair of elephants to walk side by side, others high enough for the tallest giraffes to stand in without even bending their necks.

All of a sudden, dark clouds appeared in the sky, and thunder rumbled. The people who had been laughing at Noah saw that the weather was changing and they started to head for shelter in their own homes. "Perhaps Noah isn't such a fool after all," said one. "There's a storm coming and he'll be safe and dry inside the ark."

CHILDREN'S BIBLE STORIES

Meanwhile, Noah began to gather the animals, just as God had told him to. He found a male and a female of every creature on Earth that hopped, walked, crawled or flew.

# Noah's Ark

There were giant elephants and tiny mice, stripy zebras and spotty leopards, singing birds and hissing snakes, and all the other animals, of every shape and size.

As the rain began to fall, Noah and his sons led the animals up the gangplank and into the ark. "We don't have much time," thought Noah. The sky turned black and the rain fell harder. Noah's wife, his sons and their wives made sure all the animals were safely on board, then they went into the ark. With one last glance at the world he loved, Noah went inside, too, and he shut the heavy door behind him.

### Children's Bible Stories

Outside the ark, rain poured down from the sky as thunder clapped and lightning flashed all around. Before long, great big puddles flowed into streams, the streams became rivers and lakes and then they all joined together into one giant ocean. There was no more land, as the floodwater reached over even the tallest mountains, and homes that had once been safe and dry were gone forever. Noah and the animals watched through the windows, safe and dry inside their ark.

For 40 days and 40 nights, it rained. The ark was pulled and pushed, up and down, to and fro on the rainwater ocean. Inside, the animals were frightened and Noah did his best to calm them. He trusted God and knew that all would be well in the end.

At long last, the rain stopped, just as God had said it would, and the ark lay still on the water. Then, strong winds began to blow. Little by little, the water level dropped and the tips of the mountains appeared. Soon, the ark came to rest on a mountain called Ararat, and it seemed that the ark's journey was over. Noah watched from a window as more land appeared from below the water. Then he sent a raven out into the world to see what it could find. An hour later, it came back, tired and worn, and Noah knew there was nowhere for it to land yet.

A week later, Noah sent out a dove. After a few hours, it returned with an olive twig in its beak, and Noah knew it had found at least one tree with branches above the water. It meant that Earth was drying out. "Not long to wait now," he thought. After one more week, Noah sent out the dove again. This time, the bird did not return, and Noah knew it had found a dry place to land. "Now it is safe to leave the ark," he said to his family.

# Noah's Ark

Noah flung open the doors, and the animals filed out of the ark. They all raced away in different directions, each glad to finally be free. The deer trotted off to search for fresh, green grass to eat and the ducks waddled down to the cool water to nest. The giraffes walked and the lions ran, the snakes slithered and the kangaroos hopped. Soon, they would all find new homes and raise their families on the new, dry land.

After all the animals had left the ark, Noah and his family left, too. Noah wanted to thank God, so he built an altar of stones and bowed his head to pray. "You saved me from the flood and brought me to dry land again," said Noah. "I will always be thankful."

God heard Noah's prayer and was pleased. "Now is the time for a new beginning on Earth," He said. "I bless you and your family, and I wish you well. You must have lots of children, so the world will be filled with people again. All of Earth's riches belong to you, and you must take care of them." Noah was very grateful, then God continued. "I promise that I will never send another flood to destroy the world," He said. "Look up and you will see a sign."

Noah looked up at the sky. The grey storm clouds drifted away and bright rays of sunlight shone for the first time since before the flood. As Noah watched, God made a brilliant rainbow appear, which stretched from one end of Earth to the other.

Then, God spoke again. "Whenever you see a rainbow in the sky, you will remember this day and My promise to you. Now, Noah, go and begin your new life."

Full of joy and thankfulness, Noah joined his family and the new world. Now when we see a rainbow in the sky, we remember God's promise to Noah. It's also a promise from God to us and to our beautiful world.

# The Tower of Babel

Time went by and Noah's family began to fill the world, just as God had wanted. There were grandchildren, great-grandchildren and great-great-great grandchildren. Some of the family travelled to a place called Babylonia. They learned how to make bricks and built homes for themselves. They thought they were very clever. One day, someone suggested that the Babylonians should build the tallest tower in the whole world, so that everyone would know how clever they were. It would be named the Tower of Babel. They quickly set to work.

God watched as the people built the tower. He watched the walls grow higher and higher, and it made Him very sad. He knew the people were not thinking about Him. They were thinking only about their own importance. Soon, they would become as wicked as people had been before the great flood.

God knew the people had to be able to talk to each other in order to build the tower. If they spoke in different languages, they wouldn't understand one another, and the building would have to stop. So, God made all His people speak in different languages and sent them to live in other countries around the world. The people couldn't work together, and the tall Tower of Babel remained unfinished forever.

# Abraham and Sarah

One of Noah's descendants was a man named Abraham. He was a good person who believed in God. One day, God told Abraham to leave his home. Abraham trusted God, so he and his wife Sarah did as God said.

Their journey to find a new home took several months. Then God spoke to Abraham again. "Look around you," He said. "All the land you can see will be yours forever. You will have as many children as there are stars in the sky. You will be the father of a great nation."
"How can that be?" asked Abraham. "My wife and I are too old to have children."
"Trust Me," said God. "You will have a son."

A few years later, three strangers came to Abraham's house and he welcomed them inside. "We have wonderful news for you," said the strangers. "In nine months, Sarah will have a baby son."

Nine months later, Sarah gave birth to a baby boy named Isaac. "God also promised that my family will become a great nation," thought Abraham, "and I know He always keeps His promises." Sure enough, that is exactly what happened.

# Jacob and Esau

Abraham's son Isaac grew up and married a woman named Rebekah. After they had been married for a while, Rebekah had twin boys, Esau and Jacob. Esau was Isaac's favourite child, but Rebekah loved Jacob more.

The twins grew up to be very different and didn't look at all alike! Jacob had smooth skin, but Esau's skin was hairy. As Isaac grew old, he went blind. He knew he would die soon and wanted to bless Esau as the new head of the family, since he was the older twin. But Rebekah wanted Jacob to receive Isaac's blessing, so she made a plan. While Esau was out, Rebekah dressed Jacob in Esau's clothes. She covered his arms with goatskin to make them seem hairy like his brother's. Then she sent him to Isaac.

When Isaac touched his son's hairy arm, he believed that it was Esau's, but the voice sounded wrong. "Are you really Esau?" Isaac asked his son.
"Yes, I am Esau," Jacob lied to his father. So, Isaac gave his blessing to Jacob instead of Esau.

Esau was very angry when he found out what Jacob had done. In fact, Jacob was afraid his brother might kill him, so he ran away to stay with relatives.

# Children's Bible Stories

Jacob had lied, and he had cheated his brother, but still, God didn't leave him. He had plans for Jacob, so He forgave him and helped him. One night, God came to Jacob in a dream. Jacob saw a staircase reaching up to Heaven, with angels moving up and down it. "I am the God of Abraham and Isaac," God said, "and I will make this land your home. I will bless you, your children and your children's children. I will watch over you wherever you go, and I will bring you back home."

"If You protect me and bring me safely back home as You have said," Jacob prayed, "then You will always be my God."

Soon, Jacob married and travelled home to Canaan. He was afraid that Esau was still angry with him, so he prayed to God that he and his brother would be friends. God heard his prayer, and Esau welcomed Jacob back home with open arms. Jacob had 12 sons and, in time, they grew into a great nation. Many years later, the family came to be known as the 'Children of Israel' or 'Hebrews.' God had kept His promise.

# Joseph and His Coat of Many Colours

Jacob had 12 sons, but his favourite was called Joseph. Joseph was very kind and helpful like his mother, Rachel. Before she died, Jacob had loved Rachel more than any of his other wives. He missed her very much, and Joseph reminded him of her every day. Jacob's ten eldest sons were too busy to spend time with him, and his youngest son, Benjamin, was too young. Joseph, who was the second youngest, loved sitting and talking with Jacob, and they were good friends as well as being father and son.

Jacob enjoyed showing Joseph how much he loved him. One day, he bought him a special coat, woven in bright, beautiful colours, to keep him warm while he and his older brothers looked after the sheep on the hills. "Thank you, Father," said Joseph, hugging Jacob. "I love it!"

# Joseph and His Coat of Many Colours

Joseph's brothers felt jealous because Joseph was their father's favourite. They only had plain, tattered clothes, so when they saw Joseph's new coat, they disliked him even more. One day, the brothers were walking home from the hills to help harvest the fields in Canaan, where they lived. Joseph's brothers were ignoring him and whispering mean things about him.

Joseph didn't notice that they were being unkind, and instead said, "I had a dream about the harvest last night. We each had a sheaf of golden wheat standing in the field. Mine stood tall, while your smaller sheaves bowed down to it. I think it's a message from God. What do you think?" His brothers were furious.

"Do you think you're better than us?" they asked. Joseph felt terrible. He wanted his brothers to love him, but telling them about his dream had made them hate him even more.

A short time later, Joseph had another dream that he couldn't understand. This time, he decided to tell his father and his brothers about it when they were all together at home. Perhaps his father would know what it meant. "I had another dream last night," Joseph said one evening, trying to ignore the angry looks from his brothers. "This time, the Sun and Moon and 11 stars in the glittering night sky were bowing down to me. What could it mean?"
His brothers were even more angry than before, and his father frowned, too.

"Do you think that your brothers and I will come and bow down to you?" Jacob asked. Joseph didn't dare to say any more, and Jacob didn't mention it again, but he didn't forget about Joseph's strange dream.

Joseph's brothers soon grew even more jealous of him. They left him out of everything and wanted to punish him for being their father's favourite. One day, when Benjamin was at home and they were out looking after the sheep, Jacob sent Joseph to find out how his brothers were doing. When they saw Joseph coming in his colourful coat, they felt more angry than ever. "If only we could get rid of him," said one brother.
"We could say a wild animal killed him," said another.

The others agreed. They hated Joseph so much that hurting him didn't seem like such a bad thing to do. Only Reuben, Joseph's eldest brother, tried to stop them. "No, we shouldn't kill him. We'll throw him down the well instead," he said. Secretly, Reuben thought he could rescue Joseph later when the others had calmed down. So, the other brothers ripped Joseph's beautiful coat from his back and threw him into a dry well.

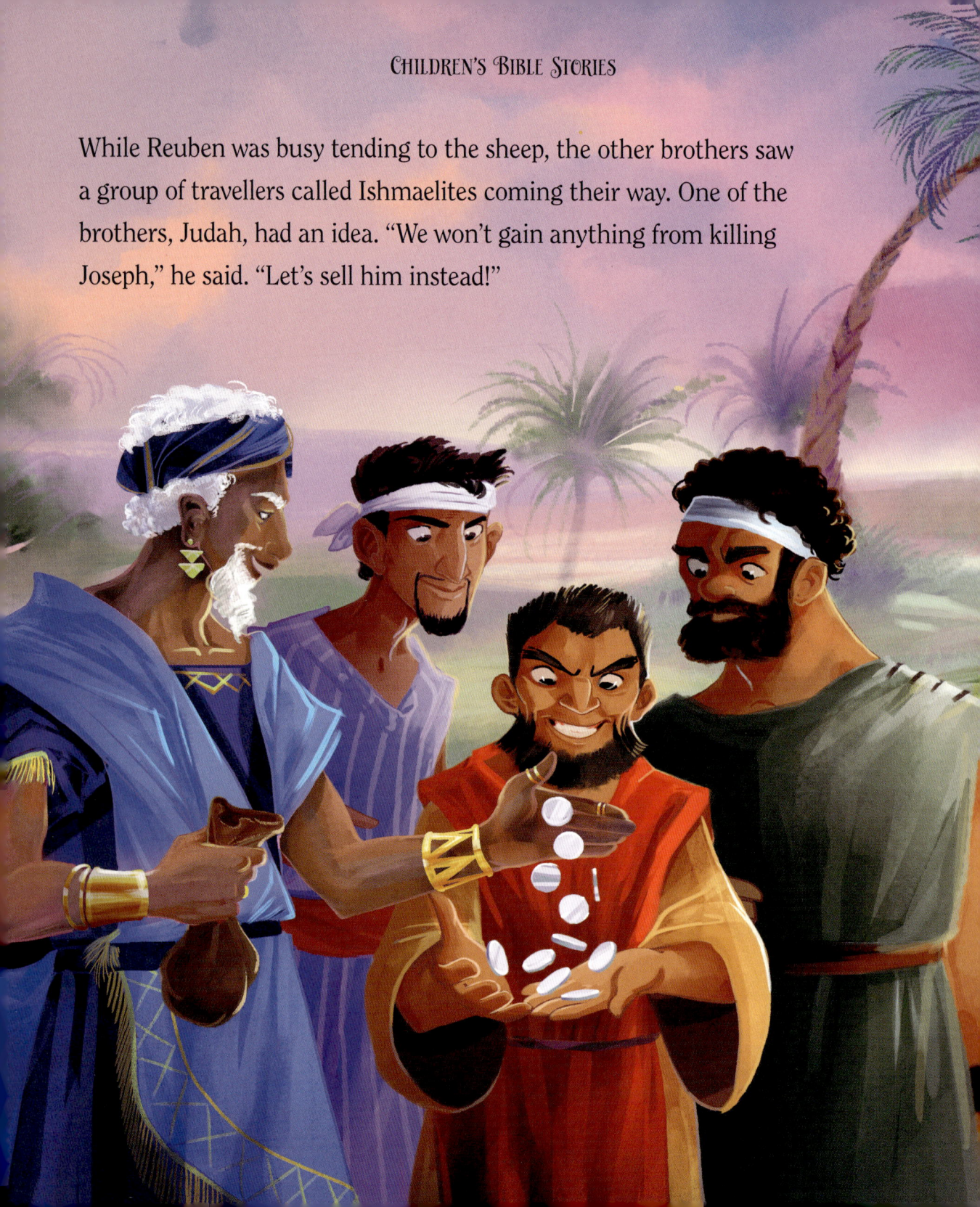

CHILDREN'S BIBLE STORIES

While Reuben was busy tending to the sheep, the other brothers saw a group of travellers called Ishmaelites coming their way. One of the brothers, Judah, had an idea. "We won't gain anything from killing Joseph," he said. "Let's sell him instead!"

So, the greedy brothers heaved Joseph out of the well and sold him for 20 pieces of silver. Shocked and hurt, Joseph was taken away from his home and his family.

Reuben was horrified when he found out what his brothers had done. "How can we explain this to our father?" he cried. "We'll make it sound like an accident," said Judah. The brothers dipped Joseph's coat in animal blood, so it looked as if a wild beast had eaten him. Then, they took it home to show Jacob.

Believing that the son he loved most was dead, Jacob was completely heartbroken. "I will mourn my beloved Joseph for the rest of my life," he said, falling to his knees and sobbing.

Joseph was taken far away to Egypt and sold to a man named Potiphar as a slave. Potiphar was an important man who worked for Pharaoh, the king of Egypt.

# Joseph and His Coat of Many Colours

"I am now a slave," Joseph said to himself. "It must be God's plan for me." At first, Joseph's life in Egypt was not too bad. Joseph knew that God wanted him to do his best, so he worked hard and became an important servant.

God blessed Potiphar's house because Joseph was there. Potiphar trusted him and everyone liked him, except Potiphar's wife. Filled with wickedness and jealousy, she told Potiphar lies about Joseph to get him into trouble. Soon, poor Joseph was thrown into prison.

# Joseph and His Coat of Many Colours

But Joseph did not feel alone in prison, because God stayed with him. He made friends with the other prisoners, too. One day, Joseph heard two prisoners talking in worried voices. They were Pharaoh's butler and baker, and they had each had a strange dream on the same night. "I know what people's dreams mean," said Joseph. "May I try to help?"

"I dreamt I saw a vine with three branches, heavy with ripe grapes," the butler said. "I squeezed the juice from the grapes into Pharaoh's cup."

"That's simple," said Joseph. "In three days, Pharaoh will set you free." Next, the baker told Joseph his dream. "I had three baskets of bread for Pharaoh," he said. "But birds swooped out of the sky and ate them all."

"I'm sorry," said Joseph, his heart aching for the man. "In three days, Pharaoh will have you killed." Before long, everything that Joseph said came true.

Two years later, Pharaoh dreamt that seven fat cows came out of the River Nile. After them came seven thin and bony cows, which ate up the fat cows. The same night, Pharaoh dreamt of seven healthy ears of corn. Another seven ears of corn sprouted, tiny and shrivelled, and swallowed up the healthy corn.

"Who can tell me what these dreams mean?" cried Pharaoh. Then, his butler remembered the man in prison who had understood people's dreams, and foreseen him being set free. Pharaoh sent for Joseph and described his dreams. "God is sending you a message," Joseph explained. "Seven years of good harvests are coming, followed by seven years of terrible famine."

# Joseph and His Coat of Many Colours

Seeing that Joseph was a man of God, Pharaoh freed Joseph and put him in charge of saving Egypt, and Joseph became rich and important. He made sure that enough grain was stored up from the good harvests to feed the Egyptian people through the hard years. Then, just as Joseph had foreseen, seven years of plenty were followed by a terrible famine, then all the people outside Egypt who hadn't stored up their grain began to starve.

Far away in Canaan, Jacob and his sons were weak and hungry. "Egypt has plenty of grain," Jacob told his sons. "Surely they can spare some for us." So, the ten eldest sons set off for Egypt, leaving Benjamin at home.

When the brothers arrived in Egypt, they were sent to see Joseph, who was in charge of selling grain to travellers. Joseph looked so different that none of the brothers recognised him, and they all bowed down before him. "It's just like my dream," thought Joseph. "At last I understand God's plan."

"We want to buy some grain," the brothers said. Joseph hoped that his brothers had changed, and thought of a way to find out.

"I think you're spies," he replied.

"No, we are all brothers," they cried. "Once there were 12 of us, but one is dead. Our youngest brother is at home with our father Jacob, in Canaan."

"Very well," said Joseph. "To prove that your story is true, bring your youngest brother to me. Otherwise, I will have you all killed." He sent the brothers home with sacks of food, but he kept his brother Simeon in Egypt to make sure that the others would return.

"This is God's punishment for the way we treated Joseph," the brothers whispered to each other. Tears came to Joseph's eyes when he saw the fear on their faces.

# Joseph and His Coat of Many Colours

At first, Jacob refused to let Benjamin go to Egypt. Since he had lost Joseph, Benjamin had become Jacob's favourite son, and he didn't want to lose him, even if it meant Simeon would have to stay in Egypt. But when they eventually ran out of food, he had to agree, and the brothers returned to Egypt with Benjamin. When they arrived, Joseph released Simeon and invited them to eat at his house. Then he filled their sacks with food, refusing to accept their money.

Secretly, Joseph asked a servant to hide a silver cup in Benjamin's sack of food. Eventually, the brothers got up to leave. "Stop!" Joseph yelled. "One of you has stolen my silver cup. Guards, search their sacks!" When the cup was found in Benjamin's sack, the brothers dropped to their knees in front of Joseph.

"Please, imprison one of us instead," they begged. "Losing Benjamin would break our father's heart." Joseph listened to them plead for Benjamin's life, and knew for certain that they had changed. Tears rolled down Joseph's cheeks as he kneeled down beside his brothers.

"Don't you recognise me?" he whispered.

When Joseph's brothers finally realised who he was, they felt so shocked and ashamed that they couldn't speak. But Joseph smiled at them. He knew that this was all part of God's plan. "I forgive you," he said. Trembling, his brothers rose and hugged him.

Then Joseph asked them to return to Canaan to tell Jacob the good news. "Bring your families and all your animals back to Egypt," he said. "I will give you the best land here."

When Jacob heard that Joseph was alive, he could hardly believe it. It wasn't until he was standing in front of his beloved son that he knew it was true. "Father!" cried Joseph, his heart bursting with joy. They wrapped their arms around each other and cried happy tears. God had brought them back together at last. Jacob settled comfortably in Egypt, in the region of Goshen, and lived to a great age.

# Joseph and His Coat of Many Colours

# MOSES

After Joseph died, life became very hard for the Israelites in Egypt. There was a new pharaoh, who was afraid that there were too many Israelites and that they would turn against the Egyptians, so he made them into slaves. Then Pharaoh ordered that all their baby boys should be killed.

One mother, Jochebed, hid her baby in a basket beside the river, where Pharaoh's daughter found him. Pharaoh's daughter wanted to save the baby's life, so she took him to live with her in the palace. She named him Moses and asked Jochebed to be his nurse. She didn't know that Jochebed was Moses's real mother. It was God's plan that the boy should grow up with his mother beside him. As Moses grew up, his mother secretly told him that he was an Israelite.

One day, Moses attacked a cruel Egyptian master who was beating an Israelite slave. He knew he would be punished by Pharaoh for helping an Israelite, so he ran away to live as a shepherd in the desert.

Many years later, God spoke to Moses. "I am the God of Abraham, Isaac and Jacob," He said. "I have seen how My people are suffering, and I want you to go back to Egypt. Tell Pharaoh that he must free the Israelites and let them leave Egypt." Moses was scared to go back to Egypt, but he could not refuse his God. So, he went to Pharaoh and asked him to let the Israelites go. Pharaoh refused.

With that, God decided to punish Pharaoh by sending terrible disasters called 'plagues' to devastate Egypt. The land was attacked by insects and frogs, the crops died and the people became very sick. Only the Israelites were saved from these plagues. But proud Pharaoh still would not free the Israelites. So, God sent the angel of death to kill the eldest son of every Egyptian family. Pharaoh's son died, too. Only Israelite families were spared.

After this, Pharaoh agreed to let the Israelites go free. But then he changed his mind and sent his soldiers to capture them again! The only way the Israelites could escape was across the Red Sea. Moses stretched out his arms and God parted the waters, so that they could cross safely into the desert on the other side. But when the soldiers tried to follow them, God made the water pour down on their heads and every one of them was killed.

The Israelites were free at last! God had kept His promise.

# Moses and the Israelites

Thanks to God, the Israelites were free from Egypt, but they were still suffering because there was no food in the desert. "We would rather have died in Egypt than starve to death here," they moaned. God heard them, and made them a promise. "I will give you meat every night and bread every day, except on the Sabbath, My day of rest," He said.

That night, a huge flock of birds appeared. They were easy to catch, so the Israelites had plenty of meat to eat. The next morning, the ground was covered with white, bread-like flakes. They appeared every morning after that and were sweet to eat. The Israelites called them 'manna'.

The Israelites had food to eat, but no water to drink. The hot sun beat down, and they became thirstier and thirstier. Moses asked God for help. "Find a rock at Mount Sinai," said God, "and hit it with your staff." When Moses did as God had told him, water gushed out of the rock. Now there was lots of cool, refreshing water for everyone to drink, and the people were happy.

Moses and the Israelites set up camp at the foot of Mount Sinai. Then, one day, God spoke to them again. "I have brought you here to be My chosen people," He said. "Will you obey Me?"

"We will," said the Israelites.

"Then I will give you ten special laws, called commandments," said God, "which show you how to serve Me and how to live together."

Two days later, thunder rumbled and lightning flashed at the top of the mountain. Together, Moses and his brother Aaron climbed all the way to the top, where God gave Moses the Ten Commandments carved on two stone tablets. These are God's ten laws:

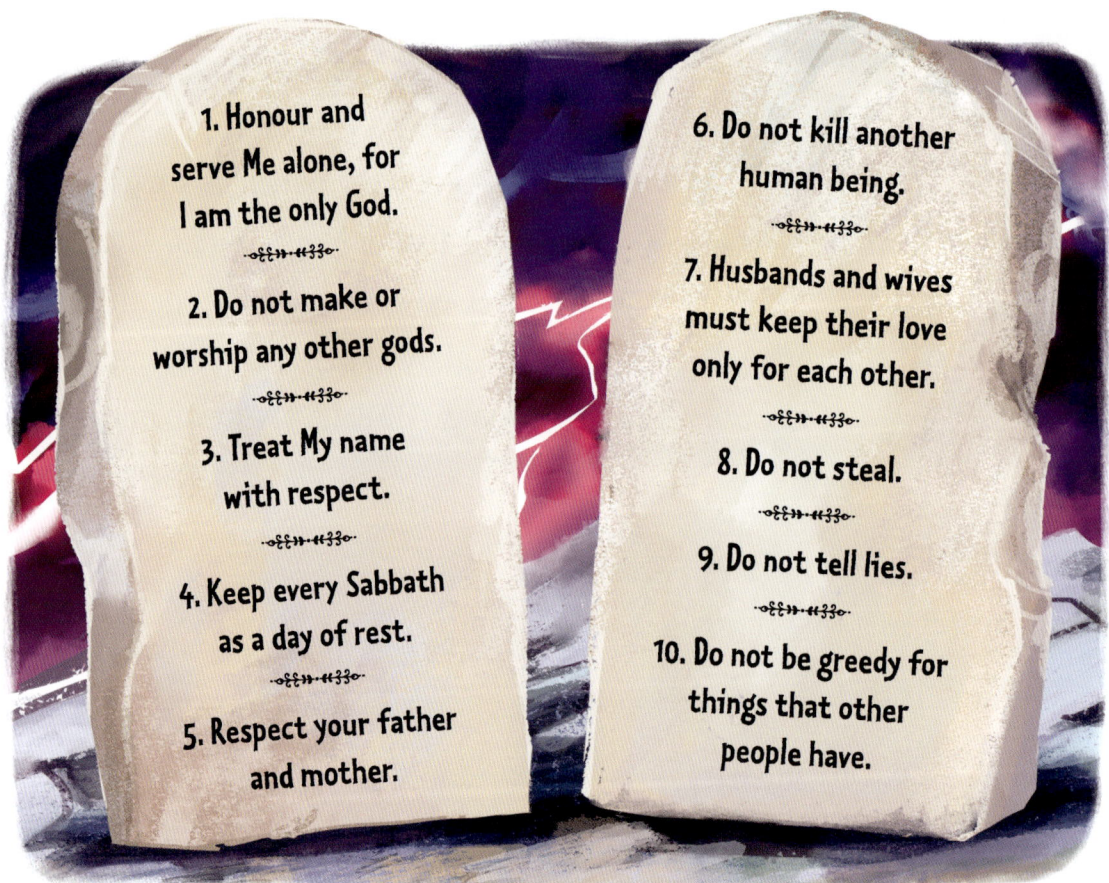

1. Honour and serve Me alone, for I am the only God.
2. Do not make or worship any other gods.
3. Treat My name with respect.
4. Keep every Sabbath as a day of rest.
5. Respect your father and mother.
6. Do not kill another human being.
7. Husbands and wives must keep their love only for each other.
8. Do not steal.
9. Do not tell lies.
10. Do not be greedy for things that other people have.

God told Moses how the laws worked, and Moses explained them to the people. He was God's special messenger, called a 'prophet'.

"God loves you," Moses told the people, "and will look after you as long as you honour Him and obey His laws."

# The Israelites Conquer Jericho

The Israelites lived in the desert for 40 years. Moses grew old and died, and God chose Joshua to be the new leader. One day, God said to Joshua, "You must cross the River Jordan into the land I promised you and capture the city of Jericho."

The Israelites travelled to Jericho. The city walls were high and thick, with strong gates, and there were soldiers on guard. It looked impossible for the Israelites to capture the city. But God told Joshua exactly what to do.

"Each day, for six days, you must march around the city. Seven priests must go first, blowing their trumpets. On the seventh day, march around the city seven times. Then, the priests must play one long note on their trumpets, and all the people must shout. The walls of Jericho will fall and the city will be yours!"

The Israelites did what God said. Down crashed the walls, and the Israelites captured the city!

This was the first of Joshua's great victories in Canaan. With him as their leader, the Israelites took over the Promised Land, and the land that God had promised to Abraham many years before.

# The First King of Israel

Many years later, God chose the prophet Samuel to lead the Israelites. Samuel was a fair leader. He loved God and he loved the honest way of life of his people. But the Israelites wanted a king, as other nations had. Even though Samuel told them that a king might not treat them well, the people insisted. So, God told Samuel, "I will give them what they want."

The young man God chose to be the king of Israel was named Saul. He was a poor Israelite whose job was to look after his father's donkeys. He had no idea that he was God's chosen king. But Samuel reassured him and told him to trust in God.

## The First King of Israel

In the beginning, Saul was a good ruler, but sadly that did not last. He soon became proud, and thought less about God and more about himself. He was so proud that, when he won battles against Israel's enemies, he thought it was because he was clever, not because God was helping him.

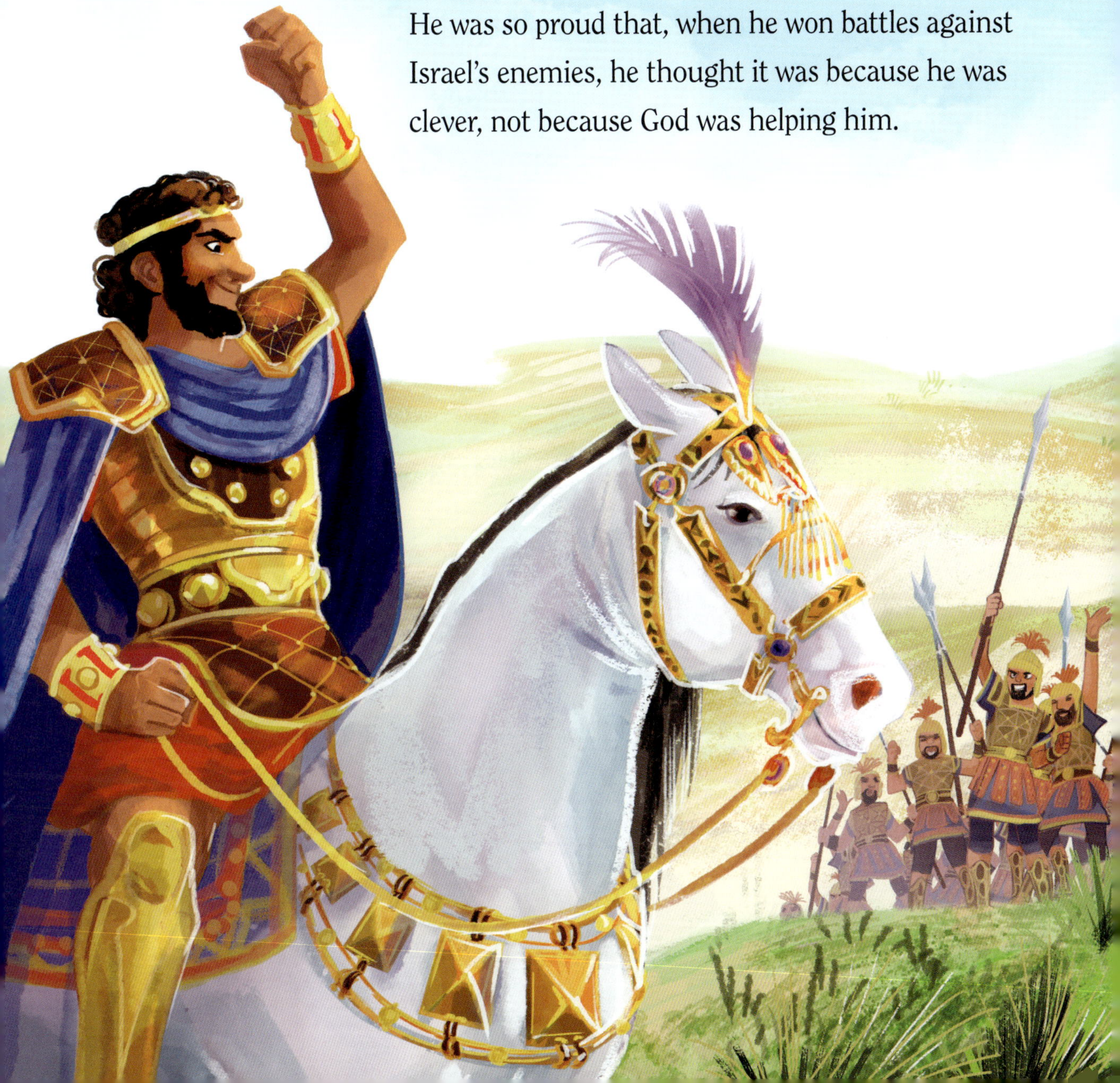

In the middle of one battle, Saul ordered that none of his soldiers should eat until they had won the fight. Anyone who ate would be killed, he said. But Saul's son Jonathan didn't hear the order. He was leading a group of soldiers on the battlefield, and none of them had eaten anything all day. He was hungry, so, when he found a honeycomb, he ate some of the sweet honey. The soldiers with him were shocked at what he had done. "Didn't you hear the king's command?" they asked. "Anyone who eats before the battle is over must be put to death."

# The First King of Israel

When proud Saul found out that Jonathan had disobeyed him, he would not go back on his word, even to save his own son's life! It was only when the Israelite people stood up to Saul that Jonathan's life was spared.

Even after this, Saul did not change his ways. He did exactly what he wanted, disobeyed God and would not listen to Samuel. He won more victories, not for God, but to satisfy his own pride and greed.

At last, God decided to find a new king to replace Saul.

# David and Goliath

God had chosen a young man named David to be the new king, and David was a shepherd. God loved David and was always with him, but there were other things God needed him to do before he took the throne.

David was a great shot with a slingshot because he used it every day to protect his father's sheep from fierce lions and bears, but David was clever in other ways, too. He was famous for playing the harp, and he was summoned to the palace to play for King Saul. "Can you soothe the king with your playing?" one of Saul's servants asked David. "He is in a terrible mood." "Of course," answered David, and began to play. Sure enough, when the king heard David's sweet music, he quickly became calmer and happier.

Far away, King Saul's battle with the Philistines was not going well. The Philistines had a fierce warrior named Goliath, who was three metres tall and stronger than an ox! He was very proud, too. "Send your greatest warrior to fight me!" sneered Goliath. "If he kills me, we will be your slaves. If I kill him, you will be ours." Only David was brave enough to take up the challenge. He knew that God would protect him.

Saul offered David his own armour and sword, but David preferred to fight without it. He picked up his slingshot, put five smooth stones in a pouch on his belt and set off to find Goliath. When he saw David, Goliath laughed.
"The Israelites's greatest fighter is a boy with a slingshot!" he cried. But David stood his ground.
"I come in the name of the God of Israel," he said. "I am not afraid!" As Goliath moved closer to attack him, David pulled one of the small stones from his pouch, put it in his slingshot, took aim and fired. The stone hit Goliath right between the eyes, making him lose his balance and fall to the ground. He was dead. When the Philistine army saw, they ran into the hills. The Israelites had won!

Years later, after Saul died, David became the new king. His greatest wish was to conquer the city of Jerusalem, so he could keep the sacred box of God's laws there, which contained the two stone tablets with the Ten Commandments on them. Eventually, he succeeded. He built a royal palace there and made Jerusalem God's city.

# King Solomon

God loved King David and promised him that his sons would always be kings. So, David told his son Solomon, "When I die, you must be a strong king, trust in God and follow His commands. Then God will keep His promise." Solomon agreed to follow his father's advice.

In time, Solomon became King and, one night, he dreamt that God asked him, "What do you need from Me?"
Solomon replied, "I am very young to rule over so many people. Please give me wisdom to make right and true decisions." This answer pleased God, and He gave Solomon more wisdom and understanding than anyone had ever had before.

Solomon was a good king in the beginning, and he made Israel rich and peaceful. But over the years, he changed. He became greedy and proud and, even worse, he did not stay faithful to God.

Solomon had to be punished. When Solomon died, God split the kingdom of Israel in two. The northern part was ruled by a man named Jeroboam, who had once been one of Solomon's servants. The southern part, a much smaller part of the kingdom, was named Judah, and was ruled by Solomon's son, Rehoboam.

105

# Daniel and the Lions

Over many years, God's people began to disobey Him. They forgot that the land they were living in was a gift from Him. So, God allowed Nebuchadnezzar, the king of Babylon, to capture Jerusalem. Many Israelites died or ran away, and there was famine in the city.

Nebuchadnezzar took many prisoners from Jerusalem back to Babylon, including a group of young men from noble Israelite families. One of them was named Daniel. He was a good man who loved God and did his best to obey Him. Even though Daniel was living in Babylon, he stayed true to God.

After some years, the Persians captured Babylon, and their leader, Darius, became King. Daniel could read and write Babylonian, and had grown very wise, so he became one of Darius's chief advisors. He served the king well, too well, perhaps, for the other advisors grew jealous and plotted against him.

Daniel prayed to God every day, and the advisors decided that this was how they would get their revenge on him. They persuaded King Darius to make a terrible new law. If a person asked any god or human being, other than the king, for anything during the next 30 days, he would be thrown into a pit of lions!

Daniel heard about the law, but kept on praying to God. His enemies were delighted. Their plan had worked! They rushed to show the king that Daniel had disobeyed him. Darius was very sad, because he liked Daniel, but Daniel had broken the law. There was no way to save him. So, at sunset, Daniel was thrown into a pit full of hungry lions.

The king felt terrible that night. He could not rest, thinking about Daniel. As soon as dawn broke, he hurried to the lion pit. He called down into the pit, "Daniel, was your god able to save you from the lions?" He thought that Daniel must be dead, so he didn't expect an answer, but to his amazement, he heard a voice!

"Your Majesty," said Daniel, "God knew that I was innocent and He has kept me safe. I have done you no wrong." Daniel was freed at once, and the men who had accused him were thrown to the lions instead. Then, Darius made a new law.

"Let everyone in my kingdom fear and respect the God of Daniel, for He is the one true, living God."

# Jonah and the Whale

Jonah lived a simple life in a small village, and he spent most of his time alone. He loved sitting outside where he could feed the birds, and he didn't like to get involved in other people's problems. One day, Jonah heard a voice that seemed to come from nowhere. "Jonah, son of Amittai, you will be My prophet," it said. Jonah jumped up and looked around, but there was no one there.

Then, the voice spoke again, and Jonah knew that it was the voice of God. "Go to the city of Nineveh and tell the people there that they have been very wicked," said God. "Explain that if they don't change their ways, I will destroy the city." Jonah was very frightened.

# Jonah and the Whale

"God wants me to leave my home and go all the way to Nineveh?" he thought. "I'm an Israelite. Why would anyone there listen to me?" He didn't care about the Ninevites, or their city, and he thought they deserved to be punished by God.

Jonah decided this must all be a mistake, so he ignored the voice. But God cannot be ignored. "Jonah, hurry up," He said. "Go to Nineveh!" So, at last, Jonah gathered some food and water for the journey, but he felt annoyed. "I don't want to get involved in anyone else's problems. I just want to be left alone," he said to himself.

# Jonah and the Whale

Finally, Jonah decided to run away so that he wouldn't have to do God's work. So, he left his home, but he did not set out for Nineveh as God had told him to. Instead, he headed for Joppa, a seaport, and got on a ship that was going to Tarshish.

"Maybe God won't notice that I am travelling in the wrong direction," Jonah thought. "By the time I get to Tarshish, it will be too late. I will be so far away from Nineveh that God will have to find Himself a new prophet!" The sun felt warm on Jonah's face and before long, he started to relax. Perhaps he really could avoid God's plan for him. The ship left Joppa, and Jonah heaved a sigh of relief.

But God did notice, and He could read Jonah's thoughts, so He knew that His prophet was trying to escape. He made the wind blow so hard that it sent Jonah's ship into the middle of a terrible storm. The ship creaked and rocked as if it would tear apart. The terrified sailors did everything they could to steer the ship away, but nothing they tried could stop the mighty waves from crashing against it over and over again.

Jonah shivered in his bunk below deck. He knew that God had sent the storm because he had not done what God had told him to. Jonah got out of his bed and staggered up to the deck. Huge waves were breaking right across the ship, and the sailors were clinging on for their lives. When Jonah saw how frightened they were, he felt very guilty. "This is all my fault!" he shouted. "I have made God angry. Throw me overboard and save yourselves."

At first, the captain refused, knowing his passenger would be drowned. But soon, the storm got even worse. The sea became wilder and the wind grew so strong that the sailors feared the ship would split in two. Desperate to save their lives, they pushed Jonah into the water, hoping the storm would end.

"God, please help me!" cried Jonah as he fell into the sea with a splash. A rush of water filled his nose and mouth, then he kicked up to the surface, coughing and spluttering. Though he was frightened, the sea was indeed growing calmer and the wind was dying down.

# Jonah and the Whale

# Jonah and the Whale

"Thank goodness," said Jonah. "Whatever happens to me, the ship and all the sailors are safe." No sooner had the storm ended, than Jonah suddenly felt himself being sucked down into the water again. "I'm going to drown!" he thought. He stretched out his arms as he was pulled further and further down into the darkness below.

# Jonah and the Whale

The next thing he knew, he could feel soft, warm walls all around him. In a panic, he kicked his legs and waved his arms, but still he was pulled further down. At last, Jonah landed on something soft and staggered to his feet. "Where am I?" he whispered.

Looking around, he saw a huge, dim cavern that smelled of fish. There was a narrow ray of light shining into the cavern and, when Jonah looked up, he saw a hole above his head. Suddenly, he felt the cavern move and, to his amazement, Jonah realised what had happened. He had been swallowed by a whale! God had seen His prophet alone and helpless in the sea. He was pleased that Jonah had sacrificed himself to save the sailors, so He had sent the whale to keep Jonah safe.

Kneeling down, Jonah spoke to God. "I am sorry for disobeying You," he said. "Please let me out of here!" But there was no reply. Jonah beat his hands against the inside of the whale, but he could not escape. So, Jonah lay inside the whale for three days and three nights. He was tired, wet and cold, and he felt weak with hunger and thirst. Worst of all, he was terrified. What if he were stuck inside the whale forever? What was God's plan for him? At last, Jonah shut his eyes and prayed. "God, I am ready," he whispered into the darkness. "I will gladly do what You asked."

Suddenly, everything started to shake, and light flooded the cavern. Jonah squeezed his eyes shut as he tumbled head over heels through the whale. "What is happening?" he cried. When Jonah opened his eyes, he was lying on soft, warm sand. The whale had spat him up onto dry land. Then Jonah heard God's voice once again. "Go to the city of Nineveh, Jonah," said God. "Do what I have asked of you."

"I will," promised Jonah. He climbed to his feet and set off right away.

When he arrived in Nineveh, Jonah was sure no one would believe he was a prophet. But he kept his promise to God and preached His message in the marketplaces. He spread God's word from slums and shacks to temples and palaces. "Turn to God and repent, or He will punish you," Jonah told the people.

# Jonah and the Whale

To his surprise, people everywhere stopped to hear him speak. They believed what he said, and God's word spread. Even the king of Nineveh listened to Jonah's message. He changed his royal robes to simple cloth to show how sorry he was for his sins. "No one in Nineveh will eat or drink until we have shown God that we are sorry for all the things we have done wrong," said the king. "I hope that He will be able to forgive us."

God heard Nineveh's prayers and was pleased with Jonah. "I will not destroy the city," He told Jonah. "They have obeyed Me, so I will show mercy."
But instead of feeling proud of helping to save the city, Jonah felt angry. "Why weren't the Ninevites punished?" he cried.
"Should you really be angry?" asked God. Jonah did not reply. He stormed out of the city, but soon, the scorching midday sun was burning down on his head.

# Jonah and the Whale

Jonah staggered to the side of the road and dropped to the ground under a bare tree. He was exhausted and furious, and there was no shelter from the sun. "I wish I had never come here," he said, fuming. "I didn't ask to get involved."

As Jonah sat there in a rage, God made fresh green leaves grow from the bare branches of the tree. It grew larger and curved itself over Jonah, until he was lying in its shade. As his body cooled down, his temper cooled, too. "Thank you, God," he murmured, as he drifted off to sleep.

At sunrise, God sent a worm to eat Jonah's tree. Its leaves shrivelled up and fell from the branches. Jonah awoke to find the sun blazing down on him again. "Why did You kill the tree, God?" Jonah raged. "It was a good tree and provided me with shelter."
"You are angry because the tree did not deserve to die," said God. "How would I have felt if I'd had to let Nineveh burn? If the tree deserves a second chance, surely My people deserve a second chance, too? And what about you, and the whale who saved you?"

Jonah bowed his head in shame. Now, he could see what God was trying to show him. "I'm sorry," whispered Jonah. God had saved the people of Nineveh, just as He had sent the whale to save Jonah, because God loves all His people.

# The Christmas Story

Long ago, in a place called Nazareth, there lived a young woman named Mary. She was engaged to be married to Joseph, a carpenter, and couldn't wait to start their life together.

One day, Mary noticed a bright, shining light. An angel had come to visit her! When Mary saw him, she was too amazed to speak, and she felt frightened. "My name is Gabriel. I have brought you a message from God," the angel said. "Don't be afraid. God has chosen you to do something special for Him. Soon, you will have a baby. He will be God's own son and he will be King. You are to call him Jesus."

Mary trusted God, so she agreed to do what He asked of her. But Joseph felt upset, because he knew he wasn't the father of the baby. "I love Mary, but I don't know if I should still marry her," he thought. So, he prayed to God for help.

God heard his prayers and, that night, He sent an angel to visit Joseph in a dream. The angel was gentle and kind. "Do not worry, Joseph," he said. "You should marry Mary and love her as your wife. She is the most special of women, chosen by God to be the mother of His son. The baby will be named Jesus, which means 'saviour', because he will save his people."

# The Christmas Story

When Joseph woke up, he decided to marry Mary right away. "I trust in God," he said to himself. So, Mary and Joseph were married, and they waited patiently for the baby to arrive.

Soon after the wedding, Emperor Augustus, who ruled over the land where Mary and Joseph lived, decided to make a list of all the people in his empire to make sure they paid their taxes. He sent messengers to every town and city in the land. "Everyone must travel back to the place they were born, so they can be counted," said the messengers.

Joseph had been born in Bethlehem, far away from Nazareth. "My wife can't travel now. She's going to have a baby soon," Joseph said to the messenger. "She should stay at home. Can we go to Bethlehem another time?" But the messenger shook his head.
"No," he said, sternly. "This is the emperor's order. You must go now."

# The Christmas Story

The journey to Bethlehem took many days. The warm sun beat down on the dusty roads, and Mary often had to stop and rest. Late one night, they finally arrived in Bethlehem. Joseph looked at Mary and saw how tired she was. "Don't worry," he said. "We'll find a place to stay for the night." But Bethlehem was packed with people who had followed the emperor's orders, and every inn they tried was full.

Eventually, Mary and Joseph reached the very last inn, but the innkeeper said, "There is no room. You'll have to try somewhere else."
"What can we do?" pleaded Mary. "My baby is coming soon."
The innkeeper was a kind man and saw how tired Mary was.
"Come with me," he said. "I have a place that might do."

# The Christmas Story

The innkeeper led them to a stable behind the inn. "I know it's not much," he said, "but it's warm and dry." Mary and Joseph looked inside. The stable was filled with animals, and the floor was covered with fresh hay.
"My baby will be safe here," said Mary. "Thank you for your kindness."

Later that night, Mary gave birth to a little boy. He was the Son of God, just as the angel had said. Joseph lined the manger with fresh hay to make a soft bed. Then Mary wrapped the baby in a blanket and laid him down gently. "We will love you and care for you, little one, and we will call you Jesus," whispered Mary.

# Children's Bible Stories

High on a nearby hillside, some shepherds were looking after their sheep. The night was dark and still, and the sheep were dozing peacefully. Suddenly, there was a dazzling light in the sky, and then an angel appeared. "What's happening?" cried the shepherds, huddling together in fear.

"Do not be afraid," said the angel. "I have the most wonderful news for you and for all the people on Earth. The Son of God has been born in Bethlehem. He is the king who will save humankind, just as God promised."

More angels appeared and sang, "Glory to God, and peace to all on Earth!" Then suddenly, the angels were gone. The shepherds looked at each other in wonder. "Can it be true?" said one shepherd to another.
"Without a doubt," the second shepherd replied. "We must go to Bethlehem and see the baby at once."

# The Christmas Story

The shepherds ran down, and through the dark streets of Bethlehem. They ran until, at last, they heard a baby's cry and found the stable where Jesus was sleeping.
"We have come to see the new king," they told Joseph, excitedly. "God sent an angel to tell us about him."

"You are all welcome here," said Joseph. So, the shepherds went inside and saw Mary with the tiny baby, who was in the manger.
"Wonderful!" said the first shepherd.
"Our saviour!" said the second, as they kneeled to gaze at him.
"We are poor. We have no gift for him," they said to Mary. "All we have to give him is our love."
"That is the very best gift in the world," said Mary. Soon, it was time for the shepherds to return to their sheep. They were so excited that they told everyone they met about the new baby king.

That same night, a new star appeared in the sky. In a faraway land, three wise men looked up and saw it. They knew it meant that something very special had happened. "The star must be a sign from God. It is shining because a new king has been born, just as He promised years ago," said the first. "We must go at once and worship him."

"Perhaps the star will lead us to the baby," said the second.

# The Christmas Story

"Let's take him the most special gifts," said the third. "Gifts fit for a king." Without delay, the wise men packed their bags, climbed on their camels and rode off towards the city of Jerusalem. They were sure they would find the new king there, at the palace.

"Where else would a king be, but in the finest of palaces?" they said to each other.

The wise men travelled across many deserts for many nights, until they finally arrived in Jerusalem. They went to the palace and asked the guards to take them to the ruler, King Herod. "Where is the new king?" they asked him. "We followed the new star that appeared on the night of his birth." King Herod was shocked. He was the only king in this land, and that was how he wanted it to stay.

"Who is this new king they speak of?" he whispered to his advisor. "A prophet once said that, one day, a new king would be born in Bethlehem," said the advisor. Herod grew worried, and planned to stop the baby from taking his throne.
"I want to worship him, too," he lied to the wise men. "Go to Bethlehem, then come back and tell me where he is."

The wise men set off into the night again. Then they travelled to Bethlehem, where the star led them to Mary, Joseph and Jesus.
"We have come to see the new king," they said to Joseph.
"You are most welcome," said Joseph. The wise men stepped inside the stable and saw Mary with her tiny baby, the Son of God. Quietly, the wise men kneeled down to give the baby their gifts.
"Here is precious gold," said the first.
"I have brought sweet-smelling frankincense," said the second.
"And this is myrrh, a healing oil," said the third.

"You will be a great king, teacher and leader, and you will save all the people of the Earth," they said to Jesus together. Then, the wise men said goodbye and found a place to rest before starting their journey home.

While the wise men slept, God visited each of them in a dream. He warned them not to return to Herod. So, in the morning, the wise men went straight home and did not return to Jerusalem. When King Herod learned that the wise men had disobeyed him, he was furious. "I am the only king!" he roared. "I will not let a baby take my throne!"

Jesus was not safe in Bethlehem now, so God sent an angel to visit Joseph while he slept. "You must wake up!" the angel said to Joseph. "Escape to Egypt, where you will be safe. Stay there until I tell you to come back." Joseph woke Mary, and they quickly loaded their belongings onto a donkey. Then, with Mary carrying Jesus tightly in her arms, they set off into the night.

Jesus was safe in Egypt, and he lived there peacefully with Mary and Joseph for some years. His parents missed their home in Nazareth, but while King Herod was alive, they knew they could never return.

Then one day, Herod died and Joseph had a dream. An angel appeared to him and said, "Joseph, it is safe for you to return home." Joseph and Mary were overjoyed. They packed up all their belongings and set off once more, with Jesus by their side.

When they arrived, they were glad to be back home at last. Joseph pointed into the distance and showed Jesus their little house.

"This is Nazareth, the town where you will grow up," he said with a smile. "Welcome home, Jesus!"

# Jesus Visits the Temple

When Jesus was 12 years old, Mary and Joseph took him to Jerusalem for the Festival of Passover. The celebrations lasted a whole week. After the festival, everyone began the long journey back to Nazareth. Mary and Joseph were walking with many other people and, at the end of the day, they realised that they hadn't seen Jesus for a long while. They searched for him, but he was nowhere to be seen. So, they hurried back to Jerusalem, hoping to find him there.

It was three days before they found Jesus. He was in the temple, listening calmly to the men who taught God's laws, and asking questions. Everyone was amazed at how much of the teaching he understood!
"We have been searching everywhere for you," said Mary. "We have been so worried. How could you do this to us?" Jesus was surprised.
"I'm sorry you were worried," he said, "but I felt so at home here in my Father's house that I decided to stay here."

Mary and Joseph were pleased that he was safe, and they set off again for Nazareth, with Jesus walking beside them all the way.

# Jesus is Baptised

Just before Jesus was born, Mary's cousin Elizabeth had given birth to a son named John. When John grew up, God spoke to him and said, "You will be My messenger. You will preach My word to the people." John did so, and people travelled from far and wide to hear him speak.

"God's king is coming soon," he told them. "Tell God that you are sorry for your sins. Change your ways, then He will forgive you." Many people were sorry for their sins, so John led them to the River Jordan and dipped their heads under the water. This was a sign that their sins had been washed away. It was called 'baptism'.

"Are you God's promised king?" people asked him.
"No," said John. "I am only a messenger. Someone much greater than me is coming soon."

One day, Jesus came to John and said, "Will you baptise me, too?"
They had never met before, but John knew at once that this was Jesus, God's promised king.
"You should baptise me, Lord," said John, falling to his knees.
"No, John," said Jesus. "I want the people to see me baptised and to know that it is important." So, John did as Jesus asked, and God was pleased.

# Jesus and His Disciples

One morning, as Jesus walked beside Lake Galilee, he saw two fishermen, Simon and his brother Andrew, pulling their fishing boats up onto the beach nearby. "Will you take me out onto the lake?" Jesus asked them. Simon agreed, and Jesus began to teach from the boat. People stopped to listen along the shore.

When Jesus had finished teaching, he told Simon to row further out and drop the fishing nets there. "We didn't catch any fish there all last night," said Simon, "but we will do as you ask." So, Simon and Andrew rowed out into the middle of the lake and dropped their nets. Instantly the nets were teeming with wriggling fish. There were so many that Simon thought the boat might sink. "James! John!" he called to two more fishermen nearby. "We need help!"

All four fishermen were amazed to see all the fish. They knew that they were watching something very special. Then, Jesus said to them, "Come and follow me. From now on, you will work with people, not fish." After this, Jesus called other people to follow him, too. Altogether, he chose 12 men to be his closest companions and share his work. They were called his 'disciples'.

# Jesus and His Disciples

# Jesus Feeds 5,000 People

As time passed, more and more people came to listen to Jesus. He would speak to the crowds for hours at a time. One day, Jesus was teaching by Lake Galilee. The day wore on and, by sunset, 5,000 people or more were gathered around him. It had been a long day and they were all very hungry. "Please send the people away," the disciples begged Jesus. "Tell them to walk to the farms and villages to find food."

But Jesus replied, "Why don't you give them food?" Jesus's disciple Andrew stepped forward. "This boy is offering five loaves and two fish, but that won't be enough to feed this crowd!" he said. Jesus took the loaves and fish, and thanked God for them. Then, he gave the food to the disciples, who broke it up and handed it out to the people. Everyone ate as much as they wanted and, when they had finished, the disciples gathered up 12 full baskets of leftover food. It was a miracle!

# Jesus Walks on Water

After this wonderful meal, Jesus told his disciples to climb into their boat and go to the other side of the lake, while he said goodbye to the crowd. Then, he went into the hills to pray.

Later that night as the wind got stronger, the disciples in the boat saw someone walking towards them over the water. They were terrified.
"It's a ghost!" they cried. But Jesus called to them.
"Don't be afraid," he said. "It's me."
Peter said, "If this is really you, Lord, tell me to come to you over the water."
"Come, Peter," said Jesus.

So, Peter got out of the boat and walked towards Jesus over the water. At first he kept his eyes on Jesus, but when he noticed the waves and the wind, he became afraid and began to sink.
"Save me, Lord!" cried Peter.

Immediately, Jesus reached out his hand to Peter and caught hold of him. "How little faith you have," said Jesus. "Why did you doubt me? Let's get back to the boat." As they did so, the wind stopped and the water was calm. Everyone in the boat was amazed and said to each other, "This truly must be God's son."

# The Woman at the Well

After visiting a faraway town, Jesus and his disciples travelled back to Galilee. They had to go through Samaria, and when they reached a place called Sychar, Jesus sat down for a rest at Jacob's Well. His disciples went into the town to buy food, and a woman came to the well to draw water. Jesus said to her, "Give me a drink."

The woman was startled. "Why are you talking to me? I'm a Samaritan woman. Most people don't talk to Samaritans," she said.

Usually this was true. But Jesus replied, "If you knew who I was, you would ask me for a drink and I would give you living water." The woman was very confused. She didn't understand what Jesus meant. This man, who ordinarily wouldn't speak to a Samaritan woman like her, didn't even have a bucket!
So, Jesus explained, "Everyone who drinks this water will be thirsty again. But whoever drinks the water that I give them will never have to thirst."
The woman said, "Sir, give me this water, so I won't be thirsty."

Unexpectedly, Jesus told the woman to bring her husband to the well. "I don't have a husband," she said. Of course, Jesus knew the truth about her life.
"You've been married five times, and now you live with a man you're not married to."

"I see that you are a prophet. My ancestors worshipped God on this mountain, but the Jews say that we must only worship in Jerusalem. I know the Messiah is coming and, when he does, he will explain everything to us," the woman said.

"The Messiah you are waiting for is me!" Jesus declared.

## Children's Bible Stories

The woman was amazed. She ran home and told the Samaritans the news. "I met a man who knows everything about me. Come, I think he is the Messiah!" And so, the Samaritans left the town and followed the woman back to Jacob's Well. They stayed there and listened to the man whom they believed was the Messiah.

# The Woman at the Well

"Come!" called Jesus. "If anyone is thirsty, let him come to me and drink! Whoever believes in me will overflow with rivers of living water! Let anyone who wishes take life's water free."

# CHILDREN'S BIBLE STORIES

After hearing Jesus teach, the Samaritans invited him to stay with them. He taught in their town for two days, and many people believed he really was the Messiah. They said to the woman, "Now that we have heard Jesus for ourselves, we know that he really is the saviour of the world."

# The Good Samaritan

One day, Jesus was teaching a group of people who had gathered around him. One of them knew a lot about the sacred books called the Scriptures and believed he would gain eternal life.

He tested Jesus with a question. "Master, what must I do to go to Heaven?"

"What do the Holy Scriptures say?" replied Jesus.

"Love God with all your heart and love your neighbour as yourself."

"Very good," said Jesus. "Practise this always, and you will gain eternal life."

"I understand," said the man. "But Jesus, who exactly is my neighbour?"

# The Good Samaritan

So, Jesus began to tell everyone a story about a man who once set out on a journey from Jerusalem to Jericho. On the way, the man was attacked by robbers. First, the thieves stole his money and all of his clothes, and they hurt him very badly for refusing to give them his belongings. Then, they ran away and left him, as though dead, on the hot and dusty road.

Some time later, a priest came along. When he saw the traveller lying on the road, hurt and bleeding, he thought to himself, "I'm far too busy to help," and hurried away without looking back.

# The Good Samaritan

Then a man who was a priest's assistant passed by. He was afraid when he saw the traveller lying in front of him, groaning and covered in blood. It would be a lot of work to help someone hurt so badly, so the man went on his way.

# The Good Samaritan

Much later, a man from Samaria, called a Samaritan, rode past on his donkey. He was in a hurry, and he knew that the traveller's people and Samaritans were enemies, but it was the Samaritan who stopped to help, not the priest or the priest's assistant. When he saw the poor traveller, hurt and alone, he washed and bandaged the man's wounds, then took him to the nearest inn, where he told the innkeeper he would pay for any treatment the man needed.

When Jesus had finished telling the story, he asked his followers a question. "Now tell me," he said, "who exactly was the wounded man's neighbour?"

"The one who showed kindness," said the first man, who had learned an important lesson. "He showed the kindness of a neighbour not only to a complete stranger, but to an enemy."

Jesus smiled. "Yes," he said. "Anyone, friend or enemy, deserves kindness and is your neighbour. Go and behave in the same way."

# The Hole in the Roof

When Jesus came to a town called Capernaum, the news quickly spread that he was there. Everybody wanted to meet him and hear his teachings, so when he visited a house and began preaching, such a large crowd gathered there that soon, the house was completely full.

The people who were left outside were disappointed not to meet Jesus, as there were so many who needed his help. One of those people was a man who could not walk. His friends had carried him all the way there, believing that Jesus could heal him. "How will we help you now?" they asked.

The man's friends refused to give up and soon, they had an idea. "Look!" they cried. "There are some stairs on the outside of the house, leading up to the roof. Maybe we can get inside that way?" So, they carried their friend up the stairs, all the way to the roof. The house was made of clay and the roof was flat.

# The Hole in the Roof

When they reached the top, one of the man's friends said, "Listen… I can hear Jesus talking down below." So, they decided to make a hole in the roof in hopes of reaching him. Soon, it was big enough to fit their friend through it.

Before long, the people inside the house noticed that something strange was happening. Just then, someone pointed towards the hole that had appeared above them. "There's a man coming through the roof!" she cried, squinting in the bright sunlight shining into the building.

The man's friends slowly lowered him through the hole until he appeared right in front of Jesus. When Jesus saw him, he knew how much he and his friends believed in him. Jesus was very happy, so he said to the man, "Friend, your sins are forgiven."

The man and his friends rejoiced, but not everyone in the house was happy. The religious leaders were shocked. Everyone knew only God could forgive sins! Why was Jesus speaking as if he were God? But Jesus knew what they were thinking, and said, "Is it easier for me to forgive this man's sins, or to tell him to get up and walk? But so that you know I do have the power to forgive sins…"

# THE HOLE IN THE ROOF

Then Jesus turned to the paralysed man and said, "Get up and go home." To everybody's surprise, the man got up and walked! Everyone was completely amazed, even those who were unhappy with Jesus. They praised God for a miracle of the kind no one had ever seen before!

# The Lost Sheep

The tax collectors and sinners were all gathering around to listen to Jesus. But the Pharisees and the teachers of the law muttered under their breath, "This man welcomes sinners to his table and breaks bread with them." Upon hearing this, Jesus stood up and told the group this story.

There once was a shepherd who lived up in the hills, looking after his flock of sheep. He had 100 sheep, and he loved every single one of them as if they were his own children. During the day, he helped the sheep find the best green grass so that they never went hungry, and when dangerous animals like bears and lions tried to hurt them, he was always there to protect them. Every night he counted each one of them to make sure all 100 sheep were safe.

Sometimes the sheep strayed away from the rest of the flock and wandered off to different parts of the hills. Because the shepherd loved the sheep, he always called them back home, and they usually came back to him straight away.

But one night, after calling his flock back home, the shepherd counted only 99 sheep. One of his beloved sheep was missing! He couldn't just relax, happy that 99 of his sheep were by his side. He worried about every single one of them because he loved all of them exactly the same. "I can't leave one sheep out in the cold just because the others are safe," he said.

So, the shepherd made sure his 99 sheep were safe and went to look for the one that was missing. He spent all night looking everywhere he could think of, until he was cold and weary. But he didn't give up and at last, he saw it.

# The Lost Sheep

"There you are!" said the shepherd. He was so happy he had found his missing sheep, and he lifted him up onto his shoulders and carried him back to the other 99 sheep. The shepherd breathed a sigh of relief because all 100 sheep in his flock were safe again. In just the same way, God is happy when one of His lost sinners turns back to Him! There's a great party in Heaven when just one person repents, and it's an even bigger celebration than when God sees 99 righteous people who think they don't need to change.

Then Jesus told everyone the true meaning of his story.
"God celebrates every single person who comes to Him to be forgiven. It doesn't matter who they are or what they've done!"

He said, "I am the good shepherd. I know my sheep and my sheep know me, just as the Father knows me and I know the Father. And I lay down my life for the sheep. Every single person, even the worst sinner, is important to God. He does not want even one single person to be lost. That's why God is even happier than the shepherd in the very story that these tax collectors and sinners here want to listen to. If only the teachers of the law wanted to believe in me, too!"

# Zacchaeus

When it was time to celebrate the Festival of Passover, Jesus and his disciples travelled to Jerusalem. They were going to pass through the city of Jericho, and news of their journey spread quickly. "Jesus is coming!" people cried. Everyone wanted to see the man who made lame men walk and blind men see.

A tax collector called Zacchaeus also lived in Jericho. Of course, nobody liked paying taxes to the Romans, but people especially didn't like Zacchaeus because he was dishonest as well. He made people pay more than they were supposed to, and then he kept the rest for himself. "No wonder he is so rich and we are so poor," people grumbled. When Zacchaeus heard that Jesus was coming to Jericho, he wanted to meet him, too. After all, Jesus said that in God's kingdom, all were welcome!

On the day Jesus arrived, Zacchaeus joined the crowds and hurried to the road he would pass on his way through Jericho. Zacchaeus was a short man, and with so many people lined up along the side of the road, he could not see over them, even standing on his tiptoes! Instead, Zacchaeus tried to push his way through the crowd. "Let me in!" he shouted, but no one would move to help the man they all disliked so much.

Suddenly, Zacchaeus spotted some tall trees at the side of the road, and he had an idea. "If I climb up there, I'll be able to see Jesus better than anyone in the whole crowd," he thought. So, he ran to the nearest tree, then climbed along one of the branches that was hanging over the road so he could sit in it.

Before Zacchaeus knew it, he heard clapping and cheering, for Jesus and his disciples were coming down the road. Everyone reached out to try and touch the man who they heard had performed miracles. Then, Jesus stopped underneath the tree Zacchaeus was sitting in. "Zacchaeus," said Jesus, "get down from that tree." Zacchaeus couldn't believe it. Jesus was talking to him!

# ZACCHAEUS

No one in Jericho wanted to speak to a tax collector, let alone greedy and dishonest Zacchaeus, but Jesus was doing just that. "I'm going to visit your house today," said Jesus. The crowd gasped. Jesus, the kind, honest man who healed the sick, was going to eat dinner with Zacchaeus, the dishonest tax collector!

Zacchaeus hurried home at once. All the way there, he thought to himself, "I've made such a mess of my life. How come Jesus wants to spend time with me?"

When Jesus arrived at his house later that day, Zacchaeus welcomed him graciously and made him a promise straight away. "You know all of my sins," he said. "But still, here you are, eating dinner at my house! I am going to give half of my possessions to the poor and pay back everyone twice the amount of money I have stolen." Jesus smiled at Zacchaeus. "I came looking for people who are lost, and to rescue those who know they need rescuing." And because Jesus loved him, Zacchaeus made some important changes in his life, and he was very glad he had met him.

# The Prodigal Son

There once was a man who had two sons. One day, the youngest son said to his father, "I need my share of your land. It's much too long to wait until you die. Give me my inheritance now!" His father agreed and, not long after, the youngest son took everything he had, set off for a distant, faraway country and selfishly spent all he'd been given, without a second thought for his father.

# The Prodigal Son

When the youngest son had nothing left, things got even worse, as there was a bad famine in the faraway land where he was living. He needed to earn money, so he found work feeding animals in the fields. He was so hungry that, eventually, he longed to eat even the scraps he fed to the farm animals, but no one gave him a thing.

Finally, the youngest son thought to himself, "My father's own workers have plenty of food to spare, and I'm in a faraway land, working hard and nearly starving!" So, he decided to make the long journey home and say sorry for what he had done. "I know I don't deserve to be treated like a son, but maybe, if my father is kind, he will allow me to come home and at least be treated like a servant."

He hadn't yet reached home when his father saw him, some way in the distance. His father was so happy to see his youngest son that, before he could say anything, he ran to him and gave him a big hug and a kiss, despite everything he had done. Still, the youngest son said, "Father, I have sinned against Heaven and against you. I am no longer worthy to be called your son."

To the son's surprise, his father said to his workers, "Quick! We must dress him in our best clothes, then let's have a feast and celebrate. For this son of mine was dead and is alive again!"

# The Prodigal Son

Meanwhile, his oldest son was in the field. At the end of a hard day's work, he came home to find music, dancing and celebration.
"What's going on?" he asked one of the workers.
"Your brother has returned," they replied, "and your father asked for a feast in his honour."

# The Prodigal Son

The older brother was very angry and refused to join in. "What's wrong, my son?" asked his father, when he found him outside.
"I've worked for you for years, without disobeying any of your orders," replied the oldest son. "You never gave me anything for my hard work. But when your sinful son returns, you give him a feast. It's not fair!"

"My son," replied his father, "I love you very much. I know that you are always with me, and everything I have is yours. But we had to celebrate, because your younger brother was dead. So it is right that we show happiness for finding someone who was lost, and is now found!"

Children's Bible Stories

# Jairus's Daughter

Many people gathered around Jesus to hear his teachings. Sometimes, he would even perform miracles. Once, a man named Jairus came to visit Jesus. He was ruler of the synagogue, and everyone liked and respected him.

"Please," said Jairus, "can you help my daughter?" For the 12-year-old girl was so ill, her father feared that she was about to die, and Jairus felt sure that Jesus would be able to make her well again.

# Jairus's Daughter

So, Jesus did as Jairus asked. They went as quickly as they could, but a crowd gathered around them, with many other people asking for Jesus to help them, too. Jairus waited while Jesus spoke to each and every one of them.

Before long, Jairus saw his friends coming towards him, looking very upset. "I'm sorry, Jairus, but it's too late for Jesus to help," they said. "Your daughter is already dead." Jairus was heartbroken. He knew that Jesus could have helped make his daughter better, but nobody could bring her back to life.

Then, Jesus smiled kindly and said, "Do not fear, Jairus. Just believe." Jairus felt confused, but he had faith in Jesus. So, with that, Jesus left the crowd. He and his disciples Peter, James and John went with Jairus and kept walking until they reached Jairus's house.

Inside, people were crying as they mourned the loss of the young girl. She was lying down in the middle of the room, with everyone gathered around her.
"Do not grieve," said Jesus, quietly, "for the child is only sleeping."

Silence fell on the room, and then people began to laugh. Everyone knew that the little girl was dead! She had stopped breathing and her heart was no longer beating. But Jairus believed, just as Jesus had said.

Then, Jesus took the girl by the hand and said gently, "Get up!" Before their very eyes, she immediately got up, not as if from the dead, but as though from a long and peaceful sleep. Jairus was amazed, and he was so grateful for the power and kindness of Jesus!

# Raising Lazarus

Jesus often visited the town of Bethany, where his friends Mary, Martha and Lazarus lived. Mary and Martha were sisters and Lazarus was their brother. Once, when Jesus was preaching in a faraway town, Lazarus fell ill, and his sisters were very worried about him. In fact, Lazarus was so ill, they thought he might die. "We must send someone to go and get our friend Jesus," said Mary and Martha. "He'll make Lazarus well again."

But when the messenger found him, Jesus said, "Tell my friends not to worry. This illness won't end in death." So, Jesus kept preaching, and said he would visit Lazarus soon.

## Raising Lazarus

A few days later, Jesus told his disciples that the time had come to travel to Bethany. "Lazarus has fallen asleep," said Jesus, "and I must go and wake him up." But the disciples did not understand, so Jesus told them, "Lazarus has died." The disciples were very confused. "How does Jesus know that Lazarus has died?" they whispered to each other. "And how is he going to wake him up?"

# Raising Lazarus

When they finally arrived in Bethany, they found lots of people at Mary and Martha's house. They were all very upset, and many of them were crying. The disciples asked someone what was happening, and they replied just as Jesus knew they would, "Lazarus has been dead for four days."

When her friend Jesus greeted her, Martha was heartbroken. "If you had visited us when we asked you to, our brother would not be dead," she said. But Jesus told her not to worry.
"Your brother will rise again, Martha," he replied, calmly. Martha did not understand. She thought Jesus meant that Lazarus would be alive again when he got to Heaven, so Jesus said, "I am the resurrection and the life. Whoever believes in me, though he dies, will live again."

Jesus wanted to speak to Mary about her brother, too. When he found her, she was so upset about Lazarus that she was crying very loudly when she said, "If only you had been here!" When Jesus saw how sad she was, and how sad everyone else was as well, he was overcome with grief. He felt so devastated, that he began to cry, too.

Finally, Jesus asked someone to take him to Lazarus's tomb. When he arrived at the cave, lots of people were gathered around it. Jesus asked his disciples to roll the stone out of the entrance. Martha gasped, as her brother had already been dead inside the cave for four days, but Jesus said, "If you believe, then you will see the glory of God."

# Raising Lazarus

Jesus prayed, "Father, thank you for hearing me. Please help these people to believe that You sent me." And then he said, "Lazarus, come out!"
Mary and Martha couldn't believe what Jesus was doing. After all, their brother was already dead. But sure enough as they peered into the entrance of the tomb, they saw Lazarus smiling back at them… alive and well!
His sisters rejoiced, and everyone was very happy.

Mary and Martha's brother emerged from his tomb just as Jesus told him to, but he was still wearing his burial clothes. "Help this man take off these clothes," said Jesus. Finally, Lazarus's sisters could embrace him, and the saddest of days turned into the happiest. Martha and Mary's brother who was dead was now alive!

# The Easter Story

It was a very exciting day in Jerusalem. Jesus had arrived in the city for the Festival of Passover, riding on a donkey. Cheers rang out from the crowd and palm leaves waved in the air. Everyone had come to see their king entering the city.

"God bless the king who comes in the name of the Lord!" they shouted. Everyone wanted to show their love and respect, and many people laid down palm leaves for the donkey to walk upon.

# The Easter Story

Jesus went straight to the city's temple, where he got a terrible shock. In the courtyard, people were buying goods, changing money and selling animals. It was noisy and smelly. The air was filled with the shouts of sellers and the cries of animals. Jesus felt very angry.
"The house of God is meant for prayer," he roared.
"But you have turned it into a place of greed!"

He knocked over the tables of wares, and coins fell to the ground. The sellers hurried away, making room for people to pray instead. Jesus's supporters cheered, but the chief priests were furious.
"He wants to destroy our power over the people," they whispered. The priests controlled everyone by making them feel afraid, but people listened to Jesus because he talked about love. "If only we could get rid of him," said the priests.

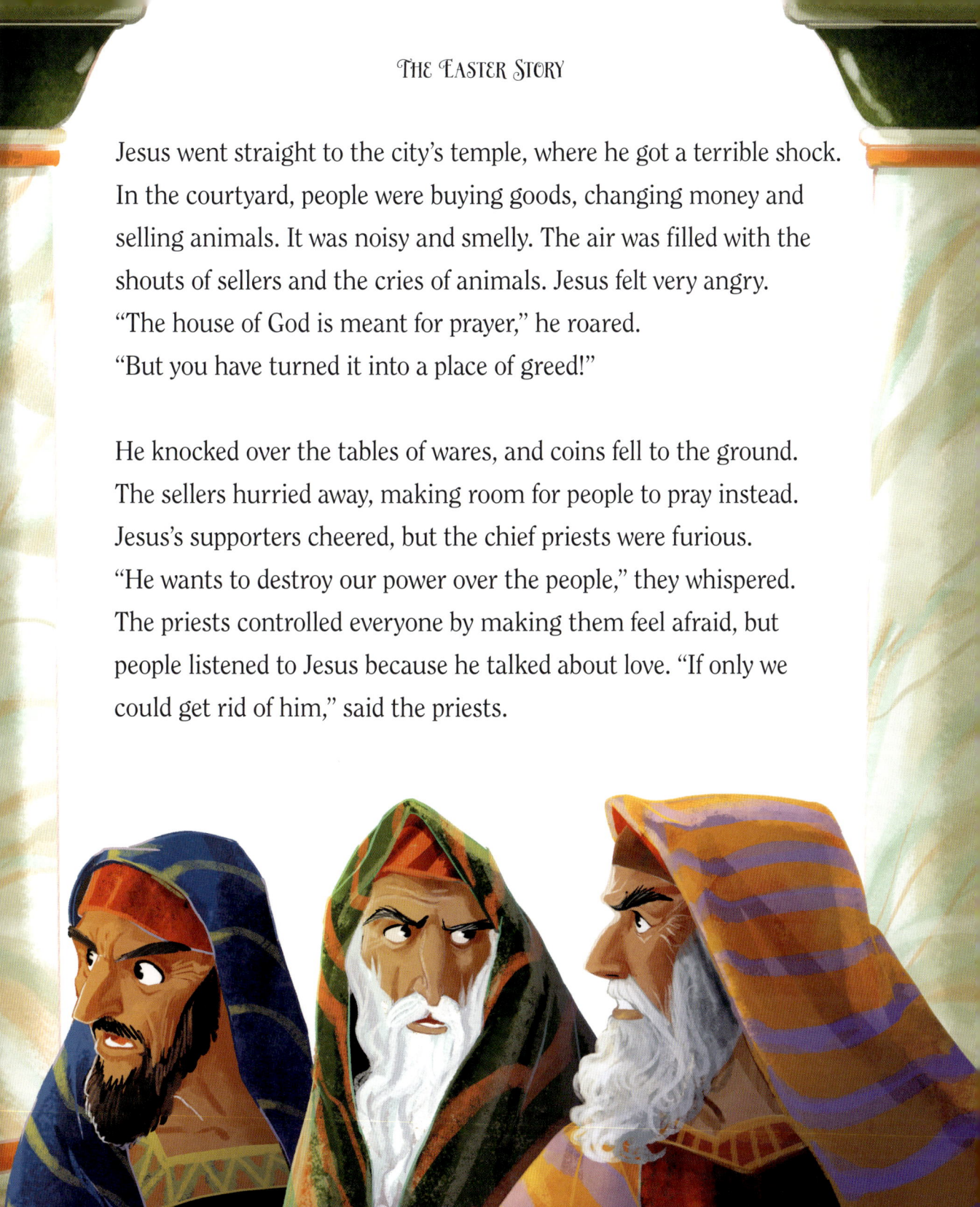

Six days before the Festival of Passover, Jesus and his disciples went to stay with some friends. While they sat around the table to eat, a woman opened a jar of expensive perfumed oil. Then, the woman began to rub the oil on Jesus's head. "You could have sold that and given the money to the poor," snapped Judas, one of Jesus's disciples. "Leave her alone, Judas," said Jesus. "She is just being kind."

Judas felt angry with Jesus, and this soon turned him bitter and evil. He knew that the chief priests didn't like Jesus, and he decided to help them get rid of him. So, two days before Passover, Judas met with the priests and agreed to lead them to Jesus when he was alone. "I will kiss Jesus to show the guards who to arrest," he told the priests. In return, the priests promised to pay Judas 30 pieces of silver.

However, Jesus knew that the priests were plotting against him. He also knew that it was all part of God's plan, and that he would soon leave the world to join his Father in Heaven. But he still felt sad when he thought about what was going to happen. The evening before Passover, Jesus took some water and kneeled in front of each of his 12 disciples in turn. He gently washed their feet and dried them on a towel.

"Lord, you should not wash our feet," said the disciples. "You are too important."
"No one is more important than anyone else," said Jesus. "Even though I am your teacher, we are all equal because we are all God's children."

When the day of Passover finally arrived, Jesus and his disciples sat down together again to eat a very special meal. "Soon, one of you will betray me," Jesus told them. The disciples were shocked, all except Judas.

"Who will it be?" they asked, but Jesus would not say and none of them noticed Judas looking guilty. Jesus blessed the bread by saying a prayer, then broke it into pieces and handed it to his disciples.

"This bread is like my body, which will be broken," he said. "Please eat it."

# The Easter Story

To show they were part of God's family, he blessed the wine and passed the cup around so they could all drink from it. "This wine is like my blood, which will be spilled for many people," he said. "Please drink it." As they ate and drank, Jesus watched his disciples with sadness in his heart.

"Eat and drink to remember me," he said. "We won't have another meal together until we are in God's kingdom."

There was a quiet garden called Gethsemane where Jesus liked to pray. After the meal, he took Peter, James and John there to pray with him. While they rested, Jesus fell to his knees. He knew that the priests were coming for him and he felt afraid. "Father, I know what needs to happen, but it's going to be very hard," he said. "Please help me." Jesus spoke to God for a long time and his disciples fell asleep.

Soon, Judas entered the garden, followed by men armed with swords and fiery torches. "Rise!" called Jesus. "Here comes the traitor." Peter, James and John rose quickly, but it was too late. Judas walked up to Jesus and kissed his cheek. It was his signal to the guards that this was the man they should arrest. The guards grabbed Jesus by the arms and held him tightly. Peter wanted to fight, but Jesus stopped him. "My Father in Heaven will protect me," he said.

The chief priests took Jesus to Pontius Pilate, the Roman governor. The Romans were in charge of Jerusalem, so it was Pilate's job to decide what would happen to prisoners. Pilate questioned Jesus, trying to find out if he was an enemy of Rome. Pilate knew that the chief priests wanted Jesus dead, but he believed Jesus was harmless.

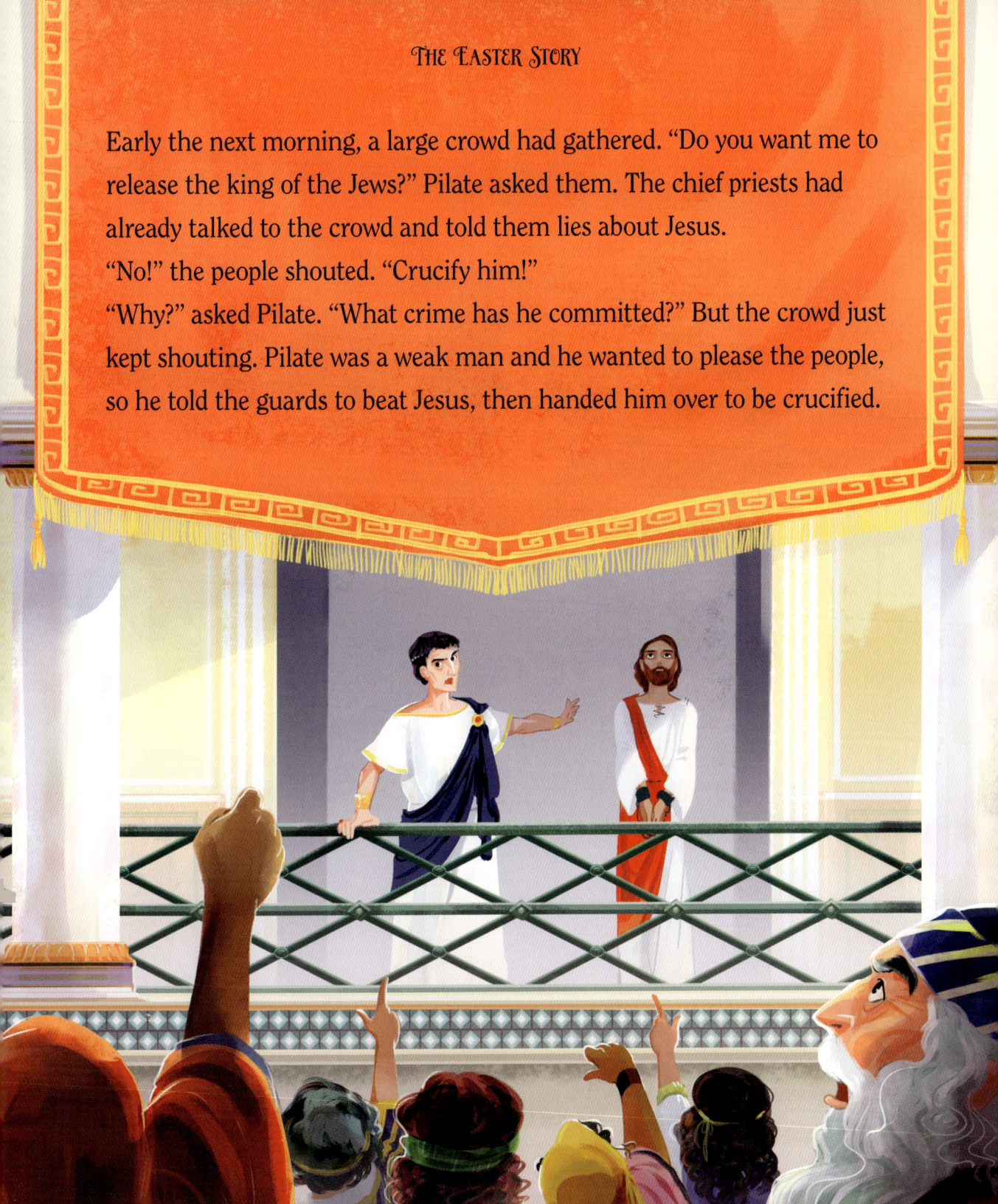

# The Easter Story

Early the next morning, a large crowd had gathered. "Do you want me to release the king of the Jews?" Pilate asked them. The chief priests had already talked to the crowd and told them lies about Jesus.

"No!" the people shouted. "Crucify him!"

"Why?" asked Pilate. "What crime has he committed?" But the crowd just kept shouting. Pilate was a weak man and he wanted to please the people, so he told the guards to beat Jesus, then handed him over to be crucified.

# The Easter Story

The soldiers dressed Jesus in a purple robe. Purple was the colour that kings wore, and they wanted to make fun of him, as they believed he'd only pretended to be a king. They even twisted together some thorns to make a crown.

"Hail, King of the Jews!" they shouted, laughing and mocking him. Then Jesus was forced to carry a heavy, wooden cross through the crowded city streets. All the way, people jeered and shouted at him. It was very different from the way he had arrived in Jerusalem.

At nine o'clock in the morning, the soldiers nailed Jesus to the cross. "Father, forgive them," whispered Jesus. "They don't understand what they are doing." Jesus was in great pain all day and it became harder and harder for him to breathe.

A crowd gathered, shouting nasty things at Jesus and making fun of him. "If you were really the Son of God, you would save yourself," they jeered. "Come down from the cross!" But Jesus did not reply. The sun went behind the clouds and the sky became dark and stormy, but the crowd and the priests kept shouting their cruel words. Finally, at three o'clock, the Son of God took his last breath.

# The Easter Story

Later that day, a Roman named Joseph took down Jesus's body from the cross, wrapped it in linen and placed it in a tomb. Then, he rolled a large, heavy stone over the entrance. Early the next morning, Mary Magdalene, one of Jesus's friends, came to visit the tomb. To her amazement, she found that the large stone had been rolled away.

Mary stepped into the dark tomb and saw that Jesus's body was gone. All that was left were the strips of linen he had been wrapped in. "He is not here," said a voice. Mary turned around and saw a man dressed all in white. She didn't realise that he was an angel, and she gasped in fear. "Do not be afraid," he said. "Jesus has risen! Go and tell his disciples." Trembling with shock and overcome with happiness, Mary fled from the tomb and ran to find Peter and John.

At first, Peter and John did not believe Mary's story. They followed her to the tomb and ran inside. "Someone has stolen the body!" they cried. "Who could have done such a thing?" They went to tell the other disciples what had happened, but Mary stayed behind.
"What shall I do?" she cried, tears running down her face. She was afraid to be there alone, but she did not want to go home, either.

"Mary," said a familiar voice. She knew Jesus's voice at once. But how could it be him? Then, the man she recognised stepped forward.
"Master!" cried Mary, falling to her knees before him.
"Tell the disciples what you have seen," said Jesus. "I will soon be with my Father in Heaven." Mary ran back to find the disciples.
"I have seen my Lord with my own eyes," she cried. "He has risen from the grave!"

# The Easter Story

CHILDREN'S BIBLE STORIES

Over the next 40 days, Jesus appeared many times to his disciples. On the Mount of Olives, near Jerusalem, he spoke to them one last time. "It is time for me to return to my Father in Heaven," he said. "Everything has happened just as He said it would. But I will always be with you."

The sun burst out from behind the clouds. As golden beams of light dazzled them, the disciples watched Jesus rise up to Heaven. Then, two angels appeared, dressed in shimmering white. "Jesus will come back to you," they promised. The disciples shared smiles of love and happiness. They knew that they would keep his words alive until Jesus returned, and they promised to spread his message of love throughout the world.